Spring Walk

To my grandchildren.

Printed in China by Toppan

Paperback Edition
23 22 21 20 19   5 4 3 2 1

Text © 2019 Virginia Brimhall Snow
Illustrations © 2019 Virginia Brimhall Snow

Published by
Gibbs Smith
P.O. Box 667
Layton, Utah 84041

1.800.835.4993 orders
www.gibbs-smith.com

Designed by Rita Sowins / Sowins Design
Gibbs Smith books are printed on either recycled, 100% post-consumer
waste, FSC-certified papers or on paper produced from sustainable PEFC-
certified forest/controlled wood source. Learn more at www.pefc.org.

Library of Congress Cataloging-in-Publication Data

Snow, Virginia Brimhall, author, illustrator.
  Spring walk / Virginia Brimhall Snow. — First edition.
      pages cm
  Summary: Grammy takes her grandchildren on a spring walk, and they learn
about the beautiful flowers that they see, and make a bouquet for their mother.
  ISBN 978-1-4236-3879-7 (hardcover)
  ISBN 978-1-4236-5393-6 (paperback)
  1. Grandparent and child—Juvenile fiction. 2. Grandmothers—Juvenile fiction.
  3. Spring—Juvenile fiction. 4. Flowers—Juvenile fiction. [1. Stories in rhyme.
  2. Flowers—Fiction. 3. Spring—Fiction. 4. Grandmothers—Fiction.] I. Title.
  PZ8.3.S674144Sp 2015
  [E]—dc23
                              2014028646

Spring Walk

VIRGINIA BRIMHALL SNOW

GIBBS SMITH
TO ENRICH AND INSPIRE HUMANKIND

crocus

I walked with Grammy
to see **flowers** today.
Tiny buds and bright
blossoms bid me to stay.

primrose

African
daisy

pansy

Some flowers smelled so **sweet**,
others made me *sneeze*.
They nodded their heads and
swayed in the *breeze*.

daffodil

I saw **yellow** daffodils,
and red tulips so tall.

tulip

I remembered we *planted* their **bulbs** last fall.

bleeding heart

There were flowers all around,

far as I could see.

forsythia

Pink, *yellow*, and **white** on bushes and trees.

peach blossom

lobelia

Bees were buzzing in the trees,
so I wanted to run.

I thought seeing *flowers* was
supposed to be fun.

California
poppy

geranium

Grammy held my hand and whispered to me,
"To make sweet fruit,
blossoms need *bees*."

calla lily

miniature hollyhock

A tiny **hummingbird** flitted
about my head.

"He *likes* flowers too," my grammy said.

forget-
me-not

I *stomped* in a **puddle** to make a big splash,

And watered some **wildflowers**
growing tall by the path.

columbine

Johnny jump-up

In the garden's soft dirt, *I dug* lots of **holes**,

Put a **plant** in each one, then *watered* with a hose.

petunia

bluebell

Grammy made furrows, and we *planted* little seeds.

"We'll *water* and watch them
and pull out the weeds."

fragaria

dianthus

phlox

"As they grow, they'll make *blossoms*
all summer long."

"May I pick some flowers now

to take to my mom?"

leopard's-bane

rose

So from Grammy's yard,
            we gathered pretty posies.

I hope Mom likes *daisies*,
        dianthuses, and *roses*.

Can you match the *flower* to the
plant or **tree** it comes from?
To check your answers, look back through the book.

phlox

petunia

bluebell

California poppy

calla lily

columbine

crocus

daffodil

dianthus

primrose

geranium

forsythia

fragaria

Johnny jump-up

leopard's-bane

miniature hollyhock

lobelia

pansy

peach blossom

bleeding heart

tulip

forget-me-not

rose

African daisy

egg carton garden

YOU WILL NEED

- 1 paper egg carton
- Scissors
- Pencil
- 2 cups potting soil
- Small bucket
- 1 seed packet (marigold works well)
- Spray bottle filled with water

DIRECTIONS

1. Cut the lid off the egg carton. Save for later.
2. With the pencil point, make a small hole in the bottom of each egg section for the water to drain out.
3. Put the potting soil into the bucket. Add just enough water to make it damp and mix well.
4. Fill all of the egg sections about three-quarters full with the damp potting soil.
5. Put two seeds in each section. Cover them with more damp potting soil to the depth on the back of the seed packet.
6. Set the egg carton with the soil and seeds inside the lid to catch drips. Put near a sunny window.
7. Moisten the soil with the spray bottle at least once a day.
8. Have fun watching the seeds sprout.
9. If more than one seed sprouts in a section, pinch it off. (This is called thinning.)
10. When the plants have two or more true leaves, and all danger of frost is past, plant them outside in the garden. Just cut the sections apart and plant cardboard and all. The cardboard will disintegrate in the dirt.

make a flower bouquet

YOU WILL NEED

- Permission from an adult to cut flowers
- Small garden clippers or old scissors
- Vase
- Flowers
- Water

DIRECTIONS

1. Cut flowers from your yard, leaving the stems long. If you don't have flowers you can cut, purchase flowers from the store.

2. Fill the vase about half full with water and set it near the edge of the table or counter you will be working on.

3. Choose a big flower and hold it in front of the vase with the end below the edge of the table. Adjust the height compared to the vase until you are happy with it. Using the clippers or scissors, cut off the end of the stem even with the edge of the counter. Even if the flower is about the right height, cut off at least $^1/_2$ inch so that the flower can get a good drink of water.

4. Carefully remove all of the leaves that are below the top of the vase. (They will get yucky in the water if you leave them on.) Put the flower in the vase. Repeat until you have all of the big flowers in place.

5. Using the same process, put all of the smaller flowers in place. When all of the flowers are in, fill the vase almost full with water using a cup.

6. Enjoy your beautiful flowers!

fun flower facts

1. African daisies close up at night, then open again the next morning.
2. Pansies like cooler weather. If they are planted in the fall, they can live under the snow all winter and bloom beautifully in the spring.
3. Bees gather nectar from flowers to make honey. While they are doing this, they pollinate fruit and vegetable blossoms, helping to make food for us.
4. Some flowers make lots of seeds, which sprout the next year as new plants. These plants that have not been planted by people are called "volunteers."
5. Petunias, roses, and geraniums need lots of sunshine, while forget-me-nots and some other flowers prefer the shade.
6. Hummingbirds drink nectar from flowers.
7. Flowers like phlox and dianthus come back each year without being replanted. These flowers are called perennials. They usually bloom for only a month or less.
8. Flowers like petunias and lobelia are called annuals. They are replanted each year, either from a plant purchased from a nursery or from seeds put directly in the ground. They usually bloom all summer.
9. Fruit trees and some flowering bushes like forsythia are covered with blossoms before they get leaves.
10. Some perfumes are made from flower blossoms.